# TRACTION ENGINES
## A Colour Portfolio

Ian Allan
60th
ANNIVERSARY

# Compiled by David Lockett & Mike Arlett

# Introduction

There is no doubt that my late father, Norman Lockett (1909–1984), had a lifelong passion for his hobby of steam railway photography. It *was* a hobby, so he *was* an amateur, but he set himself very exacting standards in the pursuit of it. There were, however, two major setbacks that Norman faced with regard to his hobby. The first was World War 2, during which he took not a single photograph. His records show that plate No 528, at Trerule (Cornwall), is dated 15.8.39 and that No 529, near Brean Road (Somerset), is dated 12.6.46; there was thus a period of nearly seven years during which his hobby was on hold. The second setback was the demise of steam on British Railways during the early to mid-'Sixties, when it was replaced, so rapidly, by diesel power.

It was around the period 1958-61 that Norman began to take additional photographs using colour transparencies. These he considered to be somewhat 'experimental' compared with his trusted black & white prints from glass-plate negatives. So, during this time, he was facing considerable change. But, most importantly, where did his future lie with regard to his hobby?

With his great friend Ivo Peters, Norman continued to seek out opportunities for steam engine/railway photography at industrial sites, preserved steam engines and railways, National Coal Board complexes and on 'specials' — steam-hauled trips organised by various steam enthusiast groups. They found out where steam engines remained on BR main lines, notably the Southern Region and in the Shap area of Cumbria, but by the time they made their last trips to Cumbria, in April and August 1967, the majority of the trains photographed at Shap were hauled by diesel locomotives.

During this time of persistent searching for steam at various locations something new appears in Norman's records. On 4 June 1967 mention is made of two photographs, Nos 240 and 241 for that year, with the description: 'road-rollers parked on the Mendips a few days before the Camerton traction-engine rally'. The next 22 photographs were taken at that rally, and the notes state, among other things, that the event was held in the field (near Camerton) of Norman's long-standing friend, Mr William (Bill) Vaughan Jenkins. There are photographs of traction engines, road-rollers, tractors, showmen's tractors and ploughing engines. This is the first reference in Norman's records to a traction-engine rally. On 7 July 1967, having photographed steam trains on the

*Front cover:* A Garrett traction engine doing what it was designed for, this threshing demonstration being a feature at the 1970 'Great Working of Steam Engines' at Stourpaine Bushes, near Blandford Forum.

*Back cover:* Aveling & Porter roller No 8361 *Lady Lucy*, built in 1914 and registered PC 9151, was new to Richmond Corporation but later worked in the Lincolnshire area until 1960. Purchased in 1970 for restoration (which took over 3,000 hours to complete), it is seen at Stourpaine Bushes in 1971 in the ownership of Messrs D. Cully and A. T. Sellwood of Calmore, near Southampton.

*Title page:* Fowler 7nhp (nominal horsepower) agricultural traction engine No 12761, built in 1911 and registered 397 TRO, was supplied new to the Forestry Commission, which used it regularly until 1945. In 1963 it was sold for scrap and ended up in Tadcaster, Yorkshire, from where it was purchased by Mr J. E. Sansome of Hinckley, who restored the engine to the fine condition seen here in September 1969.

**All photographs in this book by Norman Lockett, copyright David Lockett**

First published 2002

ISBN 0 7110 2840 0

© David Lockett & Mike Arlett 2002

Published by Ian Allan Publishing

an imprint of Ian Allan Publishing Ltd, Hersham, Surrey KT12 4RG.
Printed by Ian Allan Printing Ltd, Hersham, Surrey KT12 4RG.

Code: 0204/B2

Southern Region at Weymouth and Radipole Halt, Norman went on to his second traction-engine rally, at Yeovil. Three visits were made to traction-engine rallies in 1968, four in 1969, five in 1970 and 12 in 1971.

The whole of Norman's collection of traction-engine photographs is in colour, the colour transparency being the sole medium employed to record this new development of his hobby. Mike Arlett and I are delighted to have been asked to present a selection of these photographs in *Traction Engines — A Colour Portfolio*, the quality of which shows that Norman maintained his very high standards in this new sphere. Indeed, after a rather meagre start at Camerton, he went on to supply extensive notes for the various photographs, even adding more details at a later date, and it is this material upon which we have drawn to describe the photographs.

It would appear, then, that the answer to the question about the future of Norman's hobby after the demise of steam railway power has been answered. It was at the traction-engine rally, described variously as 'Steam Rally', 'Great Working of Steam', 'Festival of Steam', 'Steam Gala', 'Great Working of Steam Engines', 'Steam Engine & Fair Organ Rally' and 'Steam Gathering', that Norman maintained his interest both in steam and in high-quality photography of interesting mechanical objects. It is also an historical record of engineering and working machinery in common usage when steam power was King!

Finally, I should like to pay tribute to all those volunteers who helped to make the traction-engine rally possible, to those whose finance paid for the restorations, and to the folk whose practical skills made possible the restoration and repainting of derelict traction engines. Mike Arlett and I hope that this publication will, in a small way, encourage all those who continue similar work to maintain their efforts over the years to come.

*David Lockett*
Paignton, Devon
January 2002

*Right:* The occasion to which David Lockett refers in the Introduction, when his father came across these two road-rollers parked on the Mendip Hills on 4 June 1967, just a few days before the Camerton Rally. Aveling & Porter 11-ton roller No 6458 *Rowley*, built 1908, registered YA 831, and Marshall roller No 74962, built 1921, registered YA 2197.

*Above:* Burrell general-purpose traction engine No 1840 *Duke of Windsor*, built
in 1894 and later registered YA 2481. Rated at 6nhp and weighing 11 tons, it is
seen as restored by Messrs R. Willcox and C. Trott of Litton Cheney,
Dorchester, and exhibited at the Camerton Traction Engine Rally at Roundhill,
near Radstock, on Sunday 17 June 1973.

*Right:* Fowler road-roller No 18625 *Fippenny Queen*, registered TK 4285.
Built in 1929, rated at 5nhp and weighing 8 tons, it was delivered new to
Messrs Sharp of Blandford and later sold to Hine Bros of Gillingham (Dorset).
It was exhibited at the Yeovil Traction Engine Rally on 13 July 1969 as restored
by its owner, Mr A. Full of Okeford Fitzpaine, Dorset.

*Above:* Aveling & Porter tractor No 8384 *Kitty*, registered KT 2937. Built 1915, this 4nhp double-crank compound (DCC) tractor last worked commercially for Worcestershire County Council and was owned by J. Doyle of Manchester when photographed at the Lancashire Traction Engine Club Steam Engine Rally at Burtonwood Airfield, near Warrington, on 7/8 July 1973.

*Right:* Burrell showman's engine No 3847 *Princess Marina*, registered CL 4483, photographed at the Packington Steam Engine Rally on 21 September 1969. Dating from 1920, this engine was rated at 6nhp and weighed 17 tons; Norman Lockett recorded that it had been built as an experiment, using non-standard cylinders which were fed from the boiler at a pressure of 220psi. A varied working life culminated in its being cut down for use as a threshing engine. Complete rebuilding and restoration was undertaken during the 1960s under the ownership of D. C. Walker of Sutton Coldfield.

*Left:* Marshall traction engine No 52540 (but here carrying builder's plate No 52280) *Lorna*. Originally registered FU 6525 when built in 1909, this DCC 7nhp engine spent its entire working life threshing in Norfolk. Bought for preservation by Mr Torr of Gurney Slade, near Bristol, in 1967, it is seen two years later, at the Yeovil Traction Engine Rally, bearing the registration BE 7581.

*Above:* Davey Paxman agricultural traction engine No 19412, built in 1916, was rated at 7nhp and registered KE 2700. This rare example was photographed at the Medway Festival of Steam held at Great Lines, Gillingham, Kent, on 19/20 May 1973. Also prominent in this view is Aveling & Porter 10-ton roller No AD14039, built in 1930; registered JG 999 and supplied to Canterbury City Council, which retained ownership until sold in 1952, it is seen in the ownership of Mr D. Price of Ashford, Kent.

Four pictures included to illustrate the effort required to transport an exhibit to a traction-engine rally. The road-roller is 6nhp Clayton & Shuttleworth convertible No 48946 *Ironside*, built 1924 and registered YA 9576. A rare example, it was supplied new to W. W. Buncombe of Highbridge following exhibition at the Royal Show in Lincoln in 1924. In 1967 it was purchased by Sherborne Bros of Bath, which sold it on to W. ('Bill') Vaughan Jenkins of Claverton Down, Bath (a long-standing friend of Norman Lockett). Having been driven through the entrance of his home (*left*), the roller is carefully transferred onto the low-loader (*below left*) and made ready for transportation (*above right*), and finally arrives on site (*below*) — on this occasion at the Bristol Steam Traction Engine Festival at Whitchurch.

*Below:* This engine was built by Garrett as a tractor in 1919 for an estate near Canterbury, Kent. Twenty years later it was purchased by Sutton's of Beckermet, being used for threshing until 1950 and then converted to a roller; it remained in use until 1972. Builder's No 33636, this DCC engine was registered BJ 4514 and carried the name *Madge*. When photographed at the Lancashire Traction Engine Club Steam Engine Rally in July 1973 it had only recently been purchased from Sutton's by new owners R. Lee and P. Cauley of Audlem, Cheshire.

*Right:* This view, also taken at Burtonwood Airfield, the venue for the Lancashire Steam Engine Rally in July 1973, features Ransomes, Sims & Jefferies agricultural traction engine No 35247. Built in 1923, this 6nhp DCC engine spent its entire working life in the ownership of R. F. Fenn of Fraling, Essex. It was purchased from Mr Fenn in 1972 by E. Marshall of Glazebury, Lancashire, who had recently fitted new rubbers to the wheels.

*Above:* Fowler 3nhp showman's tractor No 14798 *Firefly*, built in 1919 and registered U 5313. Owned by W. Payne of Bawtry, it was photographed at 'Expo Steam', held at Battersea Park, London, on 12-14 May 1973.

*Right:* Norman Lockett visited the Stamford Traction Engine Rally held at Ryhall Grange on 23/24 June 1973. The weather was perfect for colour photography, and amongst the many pictures he took was this one featuring 1918 Ruston Proctor tractor No 52329, registered CT 5554 and owned by G. E. Stubbs of Costock.

*Left:* Ransomes, Sims & Jefferies traction engine No 15012 *The Countryman*, registered NO 4034; built in 1903 to single-cylinder (SC) design, it was rated at 7nhp and weighed 10$\frac{1}{2}$ tons. Norman Lockett photographed it at Packington on 21 September 1969 and recorded that nothing was known of its early history. In 1964, however, it had been purchased in Cambridge by Mr J. Marshall of Hockley Heath.

*Above:* Drawing admiring glances at the Yeovil Traction Engine Rally in July 1969 is Burrell 'Special Scenic' showman's road locomotive No 3483 *Perseverance II*, registered WR 9110. A DCC built in 1913, it was rated at 8nhp and weighed 19 tons, being delivered new to Harnuss of Swinton, Yorkshire, by whom it was used until sold on in 1944. It was subsequently purchased for restoration by Mr J. Gilbey of Compton Pouncefoot, Somerset.

*Above:* Sentinel 'S4'-type steam wagon No 9192, built 1935, registered CML 781. This 140bhp wagon, weighing 4 tons 19cwt, had been supplied new to the North Thames Gas Board, where it spent most of its working life. Representing the last of the Sentinel steam-wagon designs, it was powered by a four-cylinder superheated and pressure-lubricated engine. When photographed at Camerton in 1973 it was in the ownership of Mr G. B. King of Mark, Somerset.

*Right:* Clayton & Shuttleworth agricultural traction engine No 46059 of 1913, rated at 7nhp and registered CE 7943. Purchased in derelict condition in 1964 and extensively restored by Albert Deans of Baldock, it was sold on in 1968 to G. Coles of Stretford, who exhibited the engine as seen here in July 1973 at Burtonwood Airfield, near Warrington.

*Above:* Two magnificent ploughing engines at the Appleford Traction Engine Rally on 19 July 1970. Fowler No 1368 *Margaret*, registered AL 8468 and rated at 12nhp, was 100 years old when photographed and was reputed to be the oldest ploughing engine then in working order. On the right is Fowler No 2013 *Noreen*, built in 1872 and later registered AL 8463. The pair had worked together for nearly 70 years and at the time were both in the joint ownership of Messrs W. Tame and E. A. Fillmore.

*Right:* Fowler Class BB1 ploughing engine No 15222, built in 1918 and rated at 16nhp, seen at the Bristol Steam Traction Engine Rally held at Whitchurch in early May 1972. Restoration was still proceeding under the ownership of Mr C. West of Failand.

*Left:* Garrett 4nhp tractor No 33373, built in 1918 for the War Department, registered BH 8009. Most of its working life was spent in Montgomeryshire. In 1961 it was purchased for restoration by S. W. Pettifer of Motcombe, near Shaftesbury, who exhibited it at the nearby Great Working of Steam Engines, Stourpaine Bushes, on 24 September 1971.

*Below:* Clayton & Shuttleworth traction engine No 47015, built 1915 and registered BD 5483. Norman Lockett photographed this fine exhibit in June 1973 in the ownership of W. H. & L. Fowler & Sons of Holbeach Drove, a few miles to the east of the showground at Ryhall Grange, Stamford.

*Left:* Wallis & Steevens traction engine No 7764 *Wildfire*, built 1919 and registered BL 1331. An 'expansion' engine used for threshing work in Hampshire and Wiltshire, it was recorded at a steam rally held at Knowl Hill (between Reading and Maidenhead, Berkshire) in 1970.

*Right:* Burrell showman's engine No 3093 *Dreadnought*, rated at 8nhp and registered AY 9862. Supplied new in April 1909 to Hollands Amusement Caterers, Mile End, London, the engine spent its working life on the fairground circuit. It was photographed at the Lancashire Traction Engine Club Steam Engine Rally in early July 1973, at which time ownership had only recently passed to Frank Lythgoe of Warburton, Lymm.

*Below right:* Foster showman's tractor No 12509, built 1910, seen in the ownership of J. Swingler at the Stamford Traction Engine Rally held at Ryhall Grange on 23/24 June 1973.

*Left:* Fowler road-roller No 16134 *Progress*, registered U 9493, built in 1924 as a DCC and weighing 10 tons. The venue here was the Yeovil Traction Engine Rally of 7 July 1967.

*Above:* The impressive line-up of exhibits at the Appleford Traction Engine Rally in 1968 with, in the foreground, Marshall No 37690 *Old Timer*, built in 1902 and rated at 6nhp; registered BH 7373, it spent its working life in the Oxfordshire area. Next in line, Marshall No 15391 was built in 1887 and later registered BW 5249.

*Left: Sir John Fowler*, a superbly restored Fowler showman's road locomotive (No 9192) of 1902, rated at 7nhp and registered YA 44. Constructed as a road locomotive, it was later converted to a showman's. Purchased in 1971 by Mr R. M. Penny of Ston Easton, Somerset, from the Hurst Collection in Andover, Hants, it had been restored by Mr Penny and the Goold brothers of Camerton, where it is seen exhibited at the local rally held on 16/17 July 1973. Also of interest is the line-up of petrol-driven vehicles seen in the right background, themselves each today ranking as 'vintage'!

*Above:* Foden 6-ton DCC steam wagon No 11892, built 1925 and registered EC 9048. One of only three of this type of vehicle in existence, it began its working life as a three-way tipper for a quarrying contractor. It is seen at Burtonwood Airfield in July 1973 in the ownership of H. Bagot, being a part of the Levens Hall Steam Collection, near Kendal.

*Above:* This Aveling & Porter steam roller appeared at the Stamford Traction Engine Rally held at Ryhall Grange on 23/24 July 1973. Unfortunately Norman appears not to have noted down any details!

*Right:* J. & H. McLaren SC convertible No 757 was built 1902; registered AI 3029, it was rated at 6nhp and weighed 12½ tons. Supplied new to Ireland, it worked as a traction engine until 1922, when rollers were fitted. In 1940 it was converted back by the Great Northern Railway's works, but, owing to the wartime coal shortage in Ireland, was steamed only twice. Purchased for preservation in 1968, it apparently required only a few adjustments and repainting. When photographed at the Packington Steam Engine Rally in 1969 it was owned by The Rev Fred A. Coley of Redditch.

*Left:* A line-up at the Appleford Traction Engine Rally on 19 July 1970. In the foreground stands John Fowler traction engine No 13140 of 1913, rated at 7nhp, weighing 11 tons and registered Y 9955. Supplied new to an agricultural contractor in Somerset, it spent its working life in the Mendips area. Later sold to a Mr Hines of Hungerford, Berkshire, following an earlier sale into the Gloucestershire area, it was consigned to Edwards' scrapyard in Fairford but purchased in 1964 by Mr F. Simmonds of Stanford Dingley in Berkshire, who was responsible for a four-year restoration programme to the standard seen

here. (The other two traction engines feature more prominently on page 79.)

*Below:* Burrell road locomotive No 3824 was built in 1920, rated at 6nhp and weighing 10½ tons. Exhibited when new at the London Dairy Show, this engine was purchased by Messrs Shire of Thurlbear, Somerset, for threshing and timber haulage in the Taunton area, being so used until 1954. It was restored in 1968/9 and named *Lord Fisher of Lambeth* by the former Archbishop of that title who, like the owner, lived at Trent, near Sherborne, Dorset.

*Left:* Fowler 6nhp No 7459, built in 1895 and later registered BW 4506, was photographed at the Appleford Traction Engine Rally in July 1968. It had been restored three years earlier and was owned by A. V. Hall and N. Redding of Bracknell, Berkshire.

*Right:* Marshall traction engine No 36033 *Hayden Princess*, built in 1901 and registered NK 2524. A single-cylinder example rated at 7nhp and weighing 11 tons, it was photographed at the 1967 Camerton Rally in the ownership of Mr J. Miles of Charminster, Dorset.

*Right:* Again the venue is Appleford, but this time on 19 July 1970 and featuring Fowler 'R3'-class showman's engine No 15653 *Renown* of 1920, rated at 7nhp and registered CU 978. It was one of a pair of these engines delivered new to John Murphy of Gateshead to travel with his 'Proud Peacock' scenic ride, and fitted with a 'Feast' crane for lifting the scenic cars. Subsequently purchased by Mr G. R. Hawthorne, it was rebuilt over the period 1963-8.

*Left:* Aveling & Porter No 11837 *Daniel*, a 10-ton, single-cylinder road-roller built in 1926 and registered EP 3696. Sold new to J. P. Jones & Sons of Newtown, Montgomeryshire (now Powys), and later sold on to T. N. Duddleston of Whitchurch, Shropshire, it was eventually purchased and restored by A. E. Marshall of Glazebury, Lancashire, to the condition seen here at Burtonwood Airfield in 1973.

*Above:* Burrell showman's road locomotive No 3444 *His Lordship*, an 8nhp DCC built 1913 and registered CK 3403. It was purchased new by George Green of Glasgow but passed to his brother, John, in 1915. John Green & Sons later became Green Bros, owner of one of the earliest of the big scenic rides, known as 'The Golden Dragons'. Many years later, *His Lordship* came into the ownership of Silcock Bros of Warrington, and it was from this firm that the locomotive was purchased in 1949 by Mr T. Alberts of Bolton, who, presumably, added that borough's coat of arms.

*Left:* Sentinel 'S4' steam wagon No 1465, built in 1921 and registered AW 3321. It was exhibited at the 1973 Stamford Traction Engine Rally while in the ownership of R. Fearnley of Castleford, Yorkshire.

*Above:* Steam motor tractor No 33986, built 1920 by Richard Garrett of Leiston, Suffolk. Registered BJ 5601, it was rated at 4nhp and weighed 6 tons. Supplied new to Sadlers of Stourbridge, timber haulage contractors, it was taken over by Cliff James of Kingswinford and later purchased in working order by Mr A. Tinghay of Atherstone, who, at the time of this photograph at the Packington Rally in 1969, was making good use of his tractor in his boatyard.

THOMAS WOOD & SONS LTD. (Engineers & Contractors) CROCKENHILL, KENT

BP 5921

THE "BURRELL" PATENT ENGINE

*Left:* Burrell general-purpose engine No 3586 *Tam*, built in 1914 and registered BP 5921, seen at the Medway Festival of Steam in May 1973 and owned, since earlier that same year, by Thomas Wood & Sons Ltd, of Crockenhill, Kent. To the right is Aveling & Porter roller No 11423, a 5nhp compound of 1926, registered KM 2229 and named *Smokey*.

*Above:* Fowler showman's road locomotive No 15319 *Queen Mary*, registered FX 7850, seen at the Beaulieu Steam Happening held on 8 October 1972.

*Left:* Aveling & Porter convertible traction engine No 9108 *Victoria,* built in 1920 and registered BP 6711. This slide-valve DCC machine was also photographed at the Beaulieu Steam Happening on 8 October 1972.

*Above:* Aveling & Porter 10-ton, single-cylinder, piston-valve road-roller No 10555, built 1923. New to W. W. Buncombe of Highbridge, Somerset, it was later sold on to Paignton UDC (Devon) before passing to Mr E. C. Hine of Shaftesbury in 1958. It is seen here at the Yeovil Traction Engine Rally on 13 July 1969, having been purchased the previous year by Mr L. J. Casely of Trent, Dorset.

*Left:* McLaren tractor No 1837, built in 1936 and registered AAM 801. Photographed at the Stamford Traction Engine Rally held at Ryhall Grange on 23/24 June 1973, when, Norman Lockett noted, it bore the name *Bluebell* and was owned by P. Coulson of Alconbury, south of Peterborough.

*Right:* Raising steam at the Camerton Traction Engine Rally in 1967, Fowler 10-ton road-roller No 16134 *Progress*, registered U 9493, stands alongside Wallis & Steevens traction engine No 7685 *Nellie*, built in 1919 and registered HO 5587. This engine was delivered new to Geo Ewen Ltd of Petersfield, Hants, and used for threshing work until 1947; sold on to a purchaser from Liphook, where it stood derelict until 1964, it was eventually purchased and restored by S. W. Hubbuck of Shillingstone, Dorset.

*Below right:* Ransomes, Sims & Jefferies 4nhp tractor No 39127 of 1928 was bought by R. F. Giddings of Bartley, Cadnam, Hampshire, in 1970, from Messrs West of Sussex, where it was employed for most of its working life.

*Below:* Wallis & Steevens 8-ton road-roller No 8100 of 1935, rated at 10nhp and registered BAA 432. The programme for the Camerton Rally in 1973, where it was photographed, noted that this engine (owned and driven by David Antell of Shillingstone, Dorset) had worked for only three years since delivered new to Hampshire County Council. Only three of this model were constructed, the other two being then still active in South Africa.

*Right:* Foden steam tractor *Early Bird*, registered RX 1719, was new to Chawley Brickworks, where it was used to haul a trailer delivering bricks throughout Berkshire and Oxfordshire. It is seen in the ownership of Mr B. Adnams at the 1970 Knowl Hill Steam Rally.

*Above:* The 1968 Seend Traction Engine Rally, held between Melksham and Devizes (Wiltshire), attracted this exhibit, 1911 Burrell 6nhp showman's engine No 3295 *Princess Royal*, registered TA 544, owned by R. Bailey of Amesbury, Wiltshire. Obviously, Norman Lockett obtained this fine view by taking advantage of the fact that the attention of the large crowd was, at that moment in time, very firmly directed elsewhere.

*Right:* Fowler 'Tiger' 3nhp tractor No 15632, built in 1920 and registered SP 8063, was delivered new to a purchaser in Scotland. When exhibited at the 1970 Appleford Traction Engine Rally it was owned by Mr A. C. Napper.

*Left:* Wallis & Steevens oil-bath tractor No 7640, registered BL 8236 and seen at the 1973 Stamford Traction Engine Rally at Ryhall Grange, in the ownership of J. Crawley of Turvey (with an impressive line-up of other exhibits in the background).

*Above:* Another scene from the 1968 Seend Traction Engine Rally, this time featuring a Burrell 7½-ton, 6nhp SCC (single-crank compound) engine — No 2512, built in 1902 and registered TB 2846.

*Above:* Aveling & Porter Type E SC piston-valve 10-ton road-roller No 11492. Delivered new to W. W. Buncombe of Highbridge, Somerset, as No 108 in that fleet, it is seen at the Yeovil Traction Engine Rally on 13 July 1969, having been purchased two years earlier and restored by Mr D. C. Stewart of Sandford Orcas, Dorset.

*Right:* The Yeovil rally is again featured, this time on 7 July 1967. Unfortunately Norman Lockett made no notes on this Burrell traction engine, but we still wanted to include this picture because, as with many others in the book, the background is also of interest — not least the Bedford van with loud-speakers and belonging to 'Kendic Radio' of Stoke under Ham!

*Left:* Garrett Agrimotor or 'Suffolk Punch' No 33180, built in 1918 and registered BJ 4483. Norman Lockett recorded this scene at the 1970 Knowl Hill Traction Engine Rally, noting that this chain-driven tractor, named *The Joker*, had been designed for direct ploughing and was, in effect, a late attempt by builders of steam engines to counter the growing competition of the internal-combustion farm tractor. An unusual but popular exhibit, here in the ownership of Mr J. Hutchins of Ferndown, Dorset.

*Below left:* Super Sentinel timber tractor No 8777 *Old Bill*, built in 1933 and registered JB 1655. Photographed on 28 July 1968 at the Seend Traction Engine Rally, this too was owned by Mr J. Hutchins of Ferndown.

*Right:* Burrell showman's road locomotive No 3949 *Princess Mary*, an 8nhp DCC built in 1923 and registered NO 8287. This was still in active service out on the road in 1959 and was perhaps one of the best-known of all showman's engines to be found in the South of England. Supplied new to Mr Billie Nicholls and used to pull his fairground rides until the beginning of World War 2, during the war years it was stored in the open in a field. After the war and until 1959 it was in the ownership of the Presland family. The locomotive was restored over a period of eight years and repainted in 'as new' livery, albeit with some embellishments as added by her owners over the years. At the time of the photograph the owner was noted as a Commander Baldock.

*Below:* A line-up of three road-rollers and a Burrell showman's tractor exhibited at the Yeovil Traction Engine Rally on 13 July 1969. The showman's tractor is a conversion (*c*1920) from a crane tractor delivered new to the War Department in 1910.

*Right:* Foster traction engine No 14564, built in 1926 and registered FE 8055, here putting in an appearance at the 1973 Stamford Traction Engine Rally while in the ownership of R. E. Baxter of Eye Green, Peterborough.

R.BAXTER & SONS, EYE, PETERBOROUGH.

*Above:* Standing in splendid isolation at the Datchet Traction Engine Rally on 6 September 1969 is Fowler showman's road locomotive No 15652 *Pride of the North*; built in 1921, it was rated at 7nhp, weighed 17 tons and was registered CU 977.

*Right:* Norman Lockett's original notes stated only that this photograph was taken at the Packington Steam Engine Rally on 21 September 1969. He later added: 'Clayton & Shuttleworth traction engine No 44103 *Enterprise*, built 1911, SC, 7nhp, weight 10 tons, registered AL 9348'.

*Below:* A first-ever visit to the Camerton Rally in 1973 was made by this Aveling & Porter 8-ton road-roller, No 11016 *Pluisje*, built in 1924. Imported new into Holland by Akkerman & Co of The Hague, it was owned by Royal Roadbuilding Contractors Ltd in Utrecht until 1967. It was then obtained by G. van der Pol of Huizen as the first engine purchased for preservation in the Netherlands.

*Right:* Foden 6-ton 'C'-type steam wagon No 10788, built in 1922 and registered AU 6695. Purchased new for use as a brewer's dray by Jas Shipstone & Sons Ltd of New Basford, Notts, it returned to Foden in 1928 and was resold for use at quarry tips. After standing derelict near Leek for 20 years, it was purchased in 1964 by Tate & Lyle Transport Ltd, London, and completely rebuilt to represent the type of vehicle as operated by Pease & Son, carrier for Henry Tate & Sons in the early 1920s.

*Above:* Robey traction engine No 29330, built in 1910 and registered CT 4101, exhibited at Ryhall Grange, Stamford, in June 1973 in the ownership of F. B. Gibbons & Sons Ltd of Market Deeping.

*Right:* Tasker tractor No 1822, built 1920 and supplied new to Waters of Salisbury. Purchased in 1930 by Sam Smart of Warminster and converted as a showman's engine for use by Smart's for that firm's 'dodgems' fairground ride, it was sold on in 1939 and used for tree-pulling before becoming derelict. It stood thus for 18 years before purchased and restored between 1965 and 1968 by C. J. Barber and his father, and was photographed at the Datchet Traction Engine Rally on 6 September 1969.

*Above:* An impressive line-up at the Stamford Traction Engine Rally in 1973, spoilt only by the electricity pylon and associated wires.

*Left:* Garrett showman's tractor No 31193, a 5-ton, 4nhp DCC built 1912 and registered BJ 1659. Restored in 1968, it is seen here in July 1969 at the Yeovil Rally in the ownership of H. Fry & Sons of Closworth, south of Yeovil in Somerset.

*Right:* Burrell traction engine No 2662 *Attraction*, built 1904, registered AF 3531. Rated at 6nhp and weighing 9½ tons, it was supplied new to Mr Penna, a threshing contractor in the Redruth area of Cornwall. In 1955, when in the ownership of Mr Gregory of Camborne, it became the founder engine of the West of England Steam Engine Society. It was purchased in 1969 by Mr Hattam, who dismantled it and commenced restoration but then sold it on to new joint owners Paul Dove and Margaret Delisle Gray of Buckfastleigh, who completed the restoration to the superb standard seen here at the 1973 Camerton Rally.

*Left:* Plenty of variety in a line-up following the 'Grand Parade' of exhibits at the Yeovil Traction Engine Rally on 13 July 1969.

*Above:* Burrell road-roller No 4067 *Hero*, built 1927 and registered WW 1556. This 8-ton DCC roller was purchased as new by George Hall of Kirkburton, to the southeast of Huddersfield. The roller had several subsequent owners before being purchased in 1968 by J. P. Walton of Stretton, Cheshire.

*Above:* This picture was taken at the Denham Traction Engine Rally on 6 September 1970 and portrays Garrett motor tractor No 33278 *Princess Mary*, a 4nhp tractor of DCC design, built in 1918 and registered OP 4479.

*Right:* The Datchet Rally again and another small motor tractor, this time a model constructed by Burrell in 1920: Works No 3846 *Pouss Nouk Nouk*, registered AD 7782, with an unladen weight of a little under 5 tons.

*Left:* The Beaulieu Steam Happening on 8 October 1972 featured Fowler showman's road locomotive No 15657 of 1920, rated at 7nhp and registered FX 6661. Delivered new to G. J. Barnes of Portland and originally named *Kitchener*, it is here renamed *The Iron Maiden* for a film production of that name in which the engine played a principal role.

*Above:* Aveling & Porter 10-ton single-cylinder road-roller No 7632, built 1912 and new to Flintshire County Council. Discovered in 1967 at Risley, it was purchased and restored by F. & A. Dibnah of Bolton. A young Fred (later destined to become a television personality) is seen at the helm, at the Lancashire Traction Engine Club Steam Engine Rally at Burtonwood Airfield, near Warrington, in July 1973.

Aveling & Porter 10-ton single-cylinder road-roller No 8754, built in 1914 and registered VN 2370. Supplied new to North Riding County Council, this roller must have given good service, being retained for 43 years! It is pictured at Burtonwood Airfield, near Warrington, in July 1973, being exhibited by locally-based owner P. Priestner of Moore, Lancs.

Sentinel 'S4' steam wagon No 8942, built in 1934 and registered ATN 320. Purchased new by McEwan Breweries of Newcastle-on-Tyne, it was later sold to Bloxter's Quarries, Eldon, before returning to the brewery trade. Sold on again in 1942, it was converted into a tar tanker and so used until 1966 before being purchased for restoration by David Webster of Ludlow, Shropshire.

*Below:* Burrell tractor No 3894 *Saint Brannock* of 1921, rated at 6nhp and registered NX 947, spent most of its working life on road haulage in and around Barnstaple, North Devon. Purchased for restoration by Mr King of Temple Cloud, it was exhibited at some of the earliest traction-engine rallies in Devon. In 1968 it was converted to a showman's engine by Mr T. W. Gascoigne of Bodicote, near Banbury, Oxfordshire.

*Right:* Burrell agricultural engine No 3398 *Big Jack*, a 5nhp DCC built in 1912 and registered TD 264. Supplied new to Fylde Rural District Council, it was later used by Isaac Ball of Wharles, Lancashire, before being purchased in 1971 by J. F. Preston of Cabus, near Garstang, to the north of Preston.

*Left:* Foden 6-ton wagon No 13138, built in 1928 and registered AN 9568, seen at the Seend Traction Engine Rally in 1968 in the ownership of Messrs T. T. Boughton & Sons of Amersham, Bucks.

*Above:* Fowler road-roller No 16270 *Jock*, built in 1924 and registered SY 2457, at the Beaulieu Steam Happening on 8 October 1972.

*Above:* Fowler 11-ton traction engine No 11491 of 1908, rated at 7nhp and registered AH 6486, was delivered new to Davis Bros of Norfolk, where it spent its entire working life. The engine later passed through several owners until purchased by Mr J. Antell of Shillingstone, Dorset, who spent five years completely stripping down and rebuilding it to the condition seen here at the Camerton Rally in 1970.

*Left:* This Tasker Type 1A 4nhp tractor has an interesting history. Works No 1309, and built in 1904, this was an early example of a small 3-ton road tractor. Later it was converted to a road-roller and used by W. Isaac & Sons of Braunton, North Devon. In 1956 Tasker bought the engine back for its museum, only for it to be sold at the firm's dispersal sale, early in 1969. By the time it was photographed at the Yeovil Traction Engine Rally in July 1969, the new owner, Mr C. E. Porter, had reconverted the engine to a tractor and was intending for it to be used at the Sandy Bay Holiday Camp, pulling small carriages for children's rides.

Three traction engines exhibited at the 1970 Appleford Rally. On the left is Marshall No 37690 *Old Timer* of 1902, rated at 6nhp and registered BH 7373, which spent its working life in the Oxfordshire area. Next to it is 7nhp Fowler No 15710 *Tommy*, built in 1922 and registered MO 780, which spent its working life on the Berkshire Downs. On the right is 6nhp Marshall No 15391, built 1887 and later registered BW 5249, exhibited new at the Smithfield Show and sold from there to an Oxfordshire owner with whom it remained in regular use until 1949. At the time of the photograph both *Old Timer* and *Tommy* were in the ownership of Mr A. C. Napper, whilst the unnamed Marshall was owned by Mr S. J. Wharton.

# Acknowledgements

We have relied primarily on the notes written by Norman Lockett as the source of the information included in this album. Luckily Norman had also retained the official programmes of some of the rallies he attended, and these have proved a valuable source upon which we have drawn. As neither of us can be considered as anything more than an 'interested bystander', we have not sought to update any of this information. We also took the liberty of interpreting the term 'traction engine' to include the occasional picture of other modes of vintage steam vehicles, but we now understand from our publisher that this is the accepted norm! Finally, we would like to thank Keith Strickland, who — through the loan of books from his collection — usually enabled us to identify the subject matter of those few pictures which warranted inclusion but about which Norman had written very little! We hope, therefore, we have not introduced too many errors.

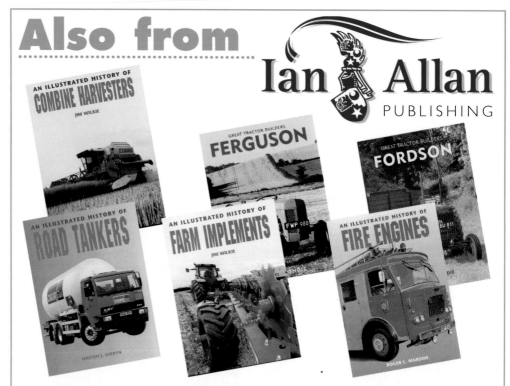